TURNING BASE

TURNING BASE
Wind Perceptions

POEMS BY
BETSY LYNCH

MILL CITY PRESS

Mill City Press, Inc.
2301 Lucien Way #415
Maitland, FL 32751
407.339.4217
www.millcitypress.net

© 2018 by Betsy Lynch

All rights reserved. No part of this publication may be reproduced, stored in a retrieval system, or transmitted, in any form or by any means, electronic, mechanical, photocopying, recording, or otherwise, without the prior written permission of the author.

Printed in the United States of America

Cover Art: Wildlife Refuge by Maro Lorimer.
marolorimer.com.

ISBN: 9781545638743

Introduction

Turning Base examines transience, love and grief, parenting and learning to let go, or not learning to let go, recovery, fear and aging, awareness of God, doubt, and power. Above all, I seek connectedness and perspective; we are not the first to live tragedy, comedy, madness. We are not alone.

The theme, **Wind Perceptions**, presented itself as the single most compelling common denominator and metaphor of my adult life; I seek awareness of weather conditions, spiritual, emotional, political, and physical. Next, I determine whether to go with the wind or against it, seek lift, or descent, cross it, relish it, use it, shelter from it, or simply accept it, palms open upward: no matter what path I choose, I can't change the wind.

Turning base, now, descending before final approach, landing, the earth reaches up gently, and perhaps it is benevolent. Or perhaps, it simply is. Listen to my story, come close. And listen to your own story in response. Maybe my story will become part of your story.

TABLE OF CONTENTS

Introduction vii

Pre-flight: Awe for those who have come before
Dis Ease of More 2
The Captain Makes Love to His Race 3
Bloom 4
Rhythm 6
_____Matters 8
Viola Organista, Homage to the Maker 10
Parenthesis 12
Prophecy 13
Good wine, hopeless trap 14
Hippy Lament 15

Pre-take-off Checklist
Shanghai Pregnant Afternoon 18
Foundation Jesus 20
Avocation 21
Dear Nikky Finney 23
#Me Too 27
Garage Sale 28

Take-off
Inspiration: First Dream Demanding Action 32
Sunday Morning 33
Cumberland Head Moment 35
Decision 36

ix

Dopamine and Periwinkle 37
September 11, 2017 39

Cruise Adjust
Humanitarian.. 42
Photograph of the Ancestress 43
Supplicant.. 44
Whiteout.. 45
Exorcism – Student Poet and Standardized Tests...................... 46
Teaching Sonnets 47
Inspiration and Censors 48
Fahrenheit 451 Poem 50
Dead Poets Society 51
Destination in Sight 52
Shanghai Teaching First Year.. 52
Classics 58
Covering Bases 59
Melting - Renga Form - Seasons 60

Storms Alter Course
Alphabets of Fear 64
Pulling the Plug.. 65
Remembering Skippy Neushaffer... 67
Pro-Choice 70
Fifty-One 71
Oratorio Society Recovered 73

Adjust Flight
Brass Quintet and Choir at Epiphany 76
Picasso meets Pachelbel on Perico's Bayou.............................. 77
Maro's Art Show 78
Jars Poetica 80

Pre-landing Checklist
Millibars... 84
How it Works Sometimes 85
Answering a Student Email 87
Disney and Dali Exhibit 89

Memories are the Pillows of Life 91
Between 93

Downwind and Slow Flight
Cessna Altitude Clock 96
Yoga practice with customer service 97
Thinking about Impeachment, Turning Base 99
Call for Peace after Election Day 101
Blood red moon: Lunar Eclipse Early Morning 102
Fireflies and Farewells: The Scotsman's Camp 103
Saturn's Sea Water Inferred 104
Sparks 106
Road Not Taken: Skyward 108

Turning Base to Final
"Alas It Was To None But Me"? 110
Pantomime on the Doomed Mango Tree 111
Sea Turtle Prescience 113
Collage on my Birthday 114
Choose Velcro 115

And So, Sometimes Just Six Words 116
Dust in the Wind, Silver Alert 119

Diode: Family Communication 122

Acknowledgements 123

Epilogue 127

Pre-flight: Awe for those who have come before

DIS EASE OF MORE

On the same day
I piloted a tiny airplane over a paradise island,

its swirling white sandbars stirred, spiraled gently by
A contemplative Zen wind-master, into aqua water,

ten thousand pastel blue greens
nuanced to cushion any anxiety,

enlighten, lift with physics-art cocktail,
my mind finally a Spanish surgeon's

antique drawing,
pen and ink rendition of retina,

minute vessels flowing intricate freestyle
rambling roots, infinite precise branches

a tree of life circuiting
sight to experience,

I heard that evening
A F16 pilot speak,

Recount his experience at atmosphere's edge, a shelf
above Saudi mountain range,

a line dividing vast black velvet, star sprinkled universe
and white desert sand mountain- shadowed dazzle.

Oh, my god I want to do that!
Aging is

childlike longing as the doors
down time's sepia corridors gradually

click shut
past gratitude.

Pre-flight: Awe for those who have come before

THE CAPTAIN MAKES LOVE TO HIS RACE

No excuse is accepted.
Measured, implacable orders given, demand response.
Watchful of competitors,
His body shifts to protect territory temporarily gained.

Breathing heavier, heat builds beneath skin,
senses, taut as rigging,
swallow sail and straining sheets,
licking wind and waves;
hips rotate as hands caress, guide the helm.

Don't hurt me, she cries, I love you, give all for you,
a small mistake made, perhaps five seconds lost,
but so much gained, we lose nothing.

A rush around the mark, the gun fires relief.
We have come
full circle again,
he smiles fulfillment.

The win is sweet, but now the next is sought;
longing, instead, to be held naked,
whispering secrets in
oil lamp shadow.

Bloom

The page vs. the stage, the poet said, battlegrounds with no turf
Incessant argument over favored theory a distraction.
Today I saw the power, the ruling dictate,
A life force beyond reckoning:
Youtube of course, what else? Youtubegooglefacebook's
Ideological censorship notwithstanding, on many
critical matters, it is always there with
middle ground no brainers,
and no brains is what it takes sometimes
to quiet the restless flying red-caped monkeys
dashing catapults inside minds' attics.

Watch: a toddler climbs playground slide steps
but this toddler has no arms, no legs,
and uses his chin and laughter,
giggling after each successful stretch
of tiny torso, past conceivable limits,
gradually getting toward the top, you see
where we're going here?

Forgeddabout your puny ass whining
somebody not giving you what you want when
you want it, some petty luxury problem; the toddler
has the stage, take your crap someplace else to
some other stage where somebody cares.
I turn my head and notice a huge pink
camellia bloomed outside my office window in
January; who imagined I'd winter in tropics?

Next, a subcontracted Ipage online- too -polite
customer service guy with an Indian accent,
too many present continuing verb forms,
and rote itismypleasuretoserveyoutoday
slowly helped

sort out my webpage issue, so I stayed
ten seconds longer, gave him a positive survey.

Perhaps to bloom is a choice, one tiny stretch at a time,
laughing at small progress,

Or perhaps it is the right youtube at the right moment,
Or perhaps it is the flying monkeys with red capes.

It's okay if you don't like this. I got what I need.

Rhythm

Everything has a rhythm, he says;
I told him he made love
the way he works with wood;
I smiled, thinking how he
creates artful curved propellers,
quick strokes, or gentle rubbing,
long strong thrusts,
a waiting time in between,
fitting parts or washing clean,
dulling the rapala knife,
its handle finger worn,
to keep wood
from hurting, a treasure
from his youth,
so now my body remembers
his camping trip wounds,
when those skills bloomed.

Or, hardening urethane, filling
in all the empty spaces, moving,
searching for anything left unfilled,
coaxing each part snuggly together,
applying sweet glue, protected from weather,
rhythm of days, sunrise to sunset,
preparing to power flight.

He explores each nerve,
maps new synapses,
a screen saver image recreates
sensation, infinite connections,
some fantastic number with no meaning, like numbers of stars,
or miles in universes, drops of water in Tampa Bay,
answers to questions like why we have

faith in wind to move boats
when we can't see it, only its symptoms.

Practice, practice, rhythm
balance, trial and error,
ebb slack and flow.
Lean. Lift.
Listen.

_____MATTERS

Laughter intrusive as blood erupting
from a slit throat,

that derisive, us-against-them sort of snark
common on tv-talking-head shows

where around a coffeetable,
people of one mind pretend

to discuss an issue upon which they
already agree to push talking points.

That, "We know
You don't" kind of laughter: a divisive virtue signal

group- think that feigns abiding superiority.
Group-think elects fringe leaders,

the deplorable rebellious outcry for reason
from those dismissed, dissed at elite coffee tables.

My poetic mechanic proclaims modern poetry
no longer "Leaves of Grass" but "leaf blowers of grass."

Perhaps more is good than you know: our women
study, sing, salve, soothe, shoot.

Practice with Chinese calligraphy, mix 'te', virtue, path of heart
with 'shen' — spirit, divine orders, return to 'tao', the oneness.

what we've missed in real laughter

the humble, self- expressive, self- effacing,
surrender, release kind of laughter

Pre-flight: Awe for those who have come before

the "I know less about life than I did
yesterday," soda -through -the -nose-snort

sort of laughter
the "welcome in, welcome home

here, sit by the fire and remember with me"
kind

Viola Organista, Homage to the Maker: Cracow, November 2013

A poem struggles through ten thousand
strange tunnels, the mind's spinning wheels
draw fine hairs upon which ideas drop,
tap, riff and rise, a challenge
to stay and attend, follow the line,
resist drink and sustenance,
resist distraction, stay to breathe,
'inspire', that verb in Latin, just as

this incredible Polish instrument maker,
pianist Zubrzycki,
five thousand hours labor,
years focused on
Codex Leonardo Da Vinci drawing
to create a string quartet sound, cello-
organ, to imagine each note tapped,
placed gently in succession, each
spinning wheel, each letter and half letter
precisely tuned, connected, arranged
as the finest grand or harpsichord,

presented in Cracow Cathedral,
a recital from the "Mona Lisa" mind
engineered, directed, scripted, down centuries,
not a technical product, but simply a sketch.

Which is the servant of a higher power, for art's
delivered miracle? The late fifteenth
century idea, or its appearance now?
What source, I wonder.
Carl Friedrich Apel's "Allegro",
an elegant stanza? Why that performance choice?

A carved dedication in gold leaf
on its deep crimson lid, in Latin, a
pronouncement of Saint Hildegard:
"Holy prophets and scholars immersed
in the sea of arts both human
and divine dreamt up a multitude
of instruments to delight the soul."

Alleluia, amen. Out of flooded tunnels,
harmony, light, precision
Out of earth, water, fire —air.

PARENTHESIS: A POEM

(Not an asterisk, no, not a period.)

More a pause, a settling quietly

waiting for the main news,

a temporary stopping off place

before the subject goes looking
for its verb.

A poem may begin secrets,

an interlude between tasks,

before or after duties, scribbled,

stuffed into a pocket,
an addition which may or
may not enrich or provide
extra details, a thrill, an irony,

(but not Essential for the survival
of your Life sentence.)

Certainly, a non- essential element.

Otherwise, if Essential, then

unprotected, un-bracketed,

the first wind might whisk

it over a cliff, (off your desk,

into a grave) silent

And ( )

PROPHECY

And so, my short story

of long ago, resting dormant
on some five- inch floppy disc, that antique precursor
of bits and bytes, cloud storage, passwords and logins, a sci-fi
"Revenge of the teacher" vignette about leading
students to the information superhighway
and abandoning them there, like poor Charlie on
the MTA who would never return no never return
and his fate still unlearned and all of that (god
who knows this anymore?),
wind shifts hardly noticed, loneliness of eternal,
unremitting, artificial, inhuman, addictive, enslaving
Connection

Was

(WTF
@
Like us on FB
Call of Duty,
Assassin's Creed, Enemy Within
Xbox360)

Prophecy

GOOD WINE, HOPELESS TRAP

Huddled heater-warm, front seat view
    of snow shrouded shipyard

canvas covers decks and spars and
    summer cabin memories
    like ghosts.

Starboard/port breakwater beacons
    blink red and green for us alone, our hosts.
Forgotten docks, dragged together
    criss-crossed like carelessly stored
    toy train tracks.

    We talk of needs and fears
and hopeless insecurities, share reveries
    of some fantasy future free of
time worries, create dream worlds
    like movie producers.

More constrained
    than teens are we whose tender intimacy
entraps, punishes; yet we are similar:
    Despite the cost, we can't go back.

Hasty departure, more than the wine
    is chilled now.
Darkness spreads across the bay.

Hippy Lament: Route 8 Cabin for Sale

Skinny-dipping in the Hudson,
my bathing suit drifted toward Manhattan:
"For sale" sign on a tiny camp
nearby, the wood-fired sauna at
Camp Dippikill, North Creek
(Nudity required), my sixth month
pregnant belly a fascination to students
they all wanted to feel the baby move
watch me nurse the other,
those flower children, they gave me
beer to make milk, enchanted
with nature's alchemy. One boy
wove wildflowers into cannibus-stem
wreath for my hair.

Road up the mountain, in Twilight Zone fog,
led to a clearing: we lived there three months
in grad school, rent free in a tent
one chore at a time, one campfire,
one sunrise, one dew-drop smoky morning,
a playful swim, a kindling gathering
a book, a flute lullaby

We moved in Autumn to a fine apartment,
the time of Watergate and baby lifts out of Saigon,
to paychecks and city-loneliness.
In spring, we took our babies to the "for sale" camp.
Oh, the dream, the dream.
We bought instead a city townhouse with soul sapping
oil bills, street sirens, screams,
sweat remodeling our equity before flight Midwest
a three -year return ticket brought temporary redemption
mountains again, but nobody's home
even in the mirror

PRE-TAKE-OFF CHECKLIST

SHANGHAI PREGNANT AFTERNOON

Thunderstorm creeps across Pudong
Expectant heads strain
hopefully toward
eastern rumble, black cloud bank,
parasols still poised against
overhead sun, merciless intensity.
Sweat has beaded on upper lip
and brow since 5 a.m.
even before Tai Chi in the park,
before scrubbing the sidewalk
before washing the children
in sidewalk pots, before
frying the bread and jawzi
"Egg McMao's" on street charcoal,
before the steamed dumplings and buns.

The storm will be welcome.
Like the 9th month of pregnancy
the wait is eternal,
the outcome uncertain.
Lotus leaves quiver
slightly in park pond,
their flowers leaning
toward each other,
metaphorical miracles
from muddy water
as Buddha said.

At last, a distant flash
rumbles, closer now.
The crane (national bird is
now construction equipment)
withdraws to a safely lower place.
Insistent bell of bicycle cart peddler

passes.
Almost silence on
Late Sunday afternoon.
Still, the Post Office is open,
and many banks. No religion,
of course, yet Sunday
remains distinct.

Could it be the treasured relief
is passing to the south?

Like the unwelcome message
from doctor to mother:

Two more weeks.

Foundation Jesus

Foundation Jesus,
bronzed nipple-length beard,
hunches over power trowel
ice boat, blades scraping cement circles
building our foundation,
walks across the wavy cement lake.
The third day, we listen
to quiet words about fish fossils
found in the Himalayas.
We listen, bend near.
He personally dug an
Adirondack mountain pond,
walked across imaginary water
on a seashell carpet snow-silver
in August moonlight.
We listen, bend near.
Works nineteen hours each day so
his daughter can study geology
at the University of New Hampshire;
he pauses, gazes skyward
for messages, prays no flood
on his new creation
at the feet of his cement block throne.

We listen, look down at our home's cradle.

Name's Thomas, actually.
Humble. Only a disciple.

Doubtful, like us.

AVOCATION (AFTER BILLY COLLINS READING, "VOCATION", IN HOROSCOPES FOR THE DEAD)

From the back of the auditorium,
a day I didn't fly my little airplane,
I heard my hero live on stage.
All these years, yes young people,
Go ahead, write something human.
I bought *Horoscopes for the Dead;*
the cover pictured an airplane,
an unusual "pusher" engine model;
it was under clouds
I saw from above yesterday.

After the reading, my timid request
for signing, and now,
bouncing from piano to computer, garden to hangar,
I attempt a letter to accompany Billy Collins' signed book
to my daughter, another teacher, for her birthday.
Will she understand?
Yes, you too can write
your heart, smile in mirrors
Wink. Start over. Study. Worship those
Moments.

Another v-tailed Bonanza zooms
past my window skyward,
while I stall for inspiration,
peruse a *Stars and Stories* book,
a gift from Christmas.

The first female astronomer, I learned,
in late 1600s, married Johannes Hevelius, to worship
at his feet and study the stars.
She became an astronomer.
A planet, Koopman 12625, was named
in her honor – her maiden name.

Stay seated, listen, read, write.
Gaze skyward into night.

On page 55 I delight to "Vocation,"
picture the night flight port light Billy
observed while the Big Dipper, he said,
"poured whatever it held into space
one big dipperful at a time"
and he discovered a secret constellation

reminded of his
true vocation:

"Keeping an eye on things/whether they exist or not/
recumbent under the stars"
whereupon I immediately knew
my new avocation:
I'll keep an eye on Billy,
worship at his feet, others too,
discover new constellations
that take even more time to explain
than why my little airplane can fly,

the whole lift, drag, thrust, air-over- wing
thing like explaining television waves

or electricity or quantum physics, neutrons zinging
through each other across continents, galaxies,

Measuring one sub-atomic particle forces
Its twin, miles away, to spin an opposite direction,
observer creating new reality

Light waves become music
only some can hear,
but just so you know:

flying **is** less risky

than writing poetry

DEAR NIKKY FINNEY: WHAT I WANTED TO SAY. . .FEBRUARY 11, 2016

(National Book Award Winner, **Head Off and Split**, 2011, Northwestern University Press)

And dedicated to my dear friend, *Dr. Daphne Kutzer, Distinguished Professor, beloved teacher and friend, SUNY Plattsburgh, rest in peace*

Last night, I absorbed your supple, story-telling hands, delicious voice-infused
imagination, rich wisdom -soaked language, "backstory" PLUS (two point oh!)

I'd forgotten how hungry I was for what you give birth to

a poem's legacy an epic child, leading generations beyond,
motion-picture camera panning multitudes, millennia,
maybe Hans Zimmer soundtrack, orchestral sweep, melody

your choices serious as court orders
your ghosts alive as neighbors

the fingers and toes, the giggles and groans, the guts and guns,
alive and juicy, whispered and shouted, birthed and nailed to historic
wooden walls, draped like Spanish moss, posted as
totems near salt marsh bone pits, my god

your truths make me weep,
separation of mother and daughter (never)
experienced in guilt
through fishmonger's vivisection reminds:
We sing our songs once we feel that blood both bequeathed
and shed

Many seek poems' birth, but few will
change their diapers, nourish through
relentless mornings, restless nights,
drive to imaginative places, collect images
feverishly, pray by attention, repetition, focus,
sever those who threaten,
nurture wildness, yet
delete distractions, deliver charges where
needed, mold, shape and discipline
emerging creations;
more often,
the gift relinquished, abandoned
to "the village" that must raise,
or judge wanting, the love- waifs
of earlier passions.

From writer's womb delivered
cherished syllable, synergized sense,
images retina implanted, inspiration
(spire, the breath of life)
a story begun, unfolding,
slippery, writhing, a tiny hand
grasps finger, mouth opens, sucking
flows milk letdown, born
from watery sleep
a new truth
I'd forgotten
my hunger.

I knew how to fly before I studied it;
flight is fear of ground dangers, entrapment:
in sleep I soar above steep mountains,
no engines nor wings necessary; I sail
across wide waters' wind, tacking
without boats, without canvas or mast or
sheets or winches, handle-less, my own rudder
moved by unseen hands, a child's book cloud-face:

Pre-take-off Checklist

puffed cheeks pursed lips blowing streams
amiable, an affable god,
judgment free
acquittal guaranteed

I meant to be a poet one day,
explore widely, share
some crone-wise woman
dancing primal heat, circling
fires in forest clearing, becoming
one moment both creation and creator;
I bought a car called ESCAPE
that sits in the driveway most days,
alas, the poems, mere starts,
ashes in air, whirling
stillborn souls in flight
adrift on clouds, still alight as
neither fire, nor wood, nor ash,
nor infant, nor wise parchment,
waiting in digital purgatory,
disappointing like a grandchild's
abandonment of piano for
video game Minecraft.
(genetic, perhaps?)

No camera projects images
from these bursts,
unfocused, double vision
angst, ADHD whims, ACOA
fear guided missives
perhaps the North Koreans
can steal for fuel
when our final darkness
descends
or doesn't
(does it)
matter?

at my age
willing to contemplate
what higher power
might offer, the stars seem
enough, my god we must
move away from starlight stealing
urban blindness, feel real darkness
to know we are not alone. Hello, darkness,
my old friend, we sang when we was young.

fill up, inspect, watch weather,
listen, set wing trim,
check gages, latches, seat belts,
throttle up, verify speed, lift rate,
fly

#Me Too

Bonfire set to burn not in effigy
the orange haired man
upwind draft smears oily ashes
on twisted faces filled with hatred
arrogance, fear echo chambers
sling mindless dehumanizing arrows at
AR-15 owners, the first who'd
protect you against harm
ask the police they'll tell you
if only you granted human status

conflating arguments an old game
guns equals religion equals pollution
equals anti-feminism equals silencing
of opposition shrieking obscenities
to replace discourse beneath
pink pussy hats we are undone again
by power hungry narcissists who
along with most leaders hire armed guards
for their children in private schools

muting the young man, survivor of Parkland
who asked CNN why his coach couldn't protect them
with his gun instead of his body?
Already, the executives atop glass ceilings
refuse network essential closed-door meetings
with women to prevent
sex harassment vitriol

the mighty Tetons rise above judgement
myths evaporate, reform in smoke drifting
above chaos, that local illusion,
past shadows of fire
where so many marionettes dance, strings
tugged by Twitter
love's gentle breeze whispers through pines

Garage Sale

1
My son, the robe of many colors I promised
Will not be sewn.
The soft striped cloth remains
Folded neatly on the table,
A symbol of what I dreamed for you
(without the sign that says
For Sale 50 cents)

How can I tell you
Who asked each day with eager eyes
When you could display your young body's new cloak
That after six winters growth
There's not enough cloth even
For one small shirt.
And if I had finished, would you now
Sob with loss like your sister for outgrown
Homemade overalls, red and blue giraffes
Prancing across yellow corduroy?
Better women save and stitch
These pieces into quilts.

2
Before they hoisted the old crib
Into the rusty pickup truck
Did I, could I have
Whispered goodbye
To that darling lamb decal
To whom I confessed my fears and sins in new motherhood?
An absurd price, my husband muttered
Feeling oddly robbed but fearing
To feel, his loss so much the same
And yet so different.
Ten times the price could not return

Those precious, hopeful fertile years,
Young LaMaze parenthood.

A half- remembered scene crept in
As the truck lumbered down the hill;
The time I leaned over the rail half the night
Listening for each new breath
Desperate for rest, but unable to close my eyes
For fear new life would slip away

3
The castle had hidden trap doors,
A pink drawbridge, a green flag on top,
A polka dot pink and yellow dragon.
I saw a woman circle slowly round it
Towing a toddler who was in love with
A tricycle behind him.

Afraid she would ask the price
I chattered over trivia, the
Weather more pressing than the pain
Remembering rainy days on the floor
Ushering little people safely across
The painted moat.

As she descended I winced
Talked of places my castle had been
Diverted her from her mission
With false animated zeal, all the while fearing
The inevitable aching loss.

Away she flew with her prey
Sulking that I could not find
The White Horse and Carriage
That used to be with my castle.
The crumpled bills she left
Dropped to the cracked cement floor as I heard:
Her child cried for the bicycle.

4
No guns! I said. No Weapons of War
In my child's hands.
By eight, his room was filled with triggers, bullets,
Metal double barrels and ominous plastic tanks.
Holsters, helmets.
Did you mean to throw these in the trash?
I'll pay you 90 cents an old man wheedled.
Anxious to protect my corner of space, I said
They're not for sale, but after he left
they had disappeared, along with all ten years
of child-made Christmas ornaments packed neatly
in a box behind the can on the shelf:
the coins he left stuck to the table.

5
My mother's Bible, a wedding gift (I hide it)
And crib sheets, footed Dr. Dentons
An old candlemaker from simpler times
(We gave candles as gifts)
A chipped platter that served
Life-giving spaghetti in graduate school
The fuzzy bear with one ear gone (she'd cried
With anxiety at the sight)
The rusty tricycle, the books from another land
Another life.

More vivid than movies, these old snapshots,
These haunting fragments of time.
I'll not be there, nor here - again.
Twenty- nine dollars and eighty- seven cents.
This currency, too, will be gone tomorrow
(Why else call it that?)

I wish the intruders away.

TAKE-OFF

Inspiration: First Dream Demanding Action

Muses come, they do
She's all winter white or beige
He's light chocolate tight belly
They take me flying out the window
At night,
In the rain to discover:
Look, there's cro-magnon skiier
All skeletal here, quick, over the snowy purple mountains,
the shadow of someone
Bringing down a knife to cut, and there,
Children gathered by the fire
Waiting for you.

Chocolate man says
I know a story when I see it
(Why do I see it too? I ask)
You have it too. Come fly with me.
We soar, winter white and beige woman, black writer man
and me, out through my bedroom window
over lake and mountains. Later,
we land on the front porch to talk;
husband intruder wants to come out,
but he's not dressed;
he's peering around the corner, angry,
wants us to be quiet, his
shoes neatly aligned by the bed.

When I awake, he is tightening
the window's lock
with a screwdriver.
If you don't keep after things
Everything falls apart,
he says.

Sunday Morning (apologies to Wallace Stevens when the Telemarketer is a Safe Haven)

Intrusions into brooding mood
whilst I pray for other relief,
Jason, calling for Septi-clean
Reassures that he is not
Selling something
(no complacencies of
the peignoir here, no
coffee and pungent oranges
just telemarketing)

Asks if I know my septic system
Needs bacteria to function
(no green cockatoo, just
dark encroachment of
that old catastrophe)
poor boy reads from a script
paid hourly, but commissions too
no doubt, think of
my own son long ago

(no holy hush of ancient sacrifice)
only this moment saved
from the pit of dark misery
(no contemplating
ancient mysteries here,
just credit card bills)
pre-holiday shouting matches
over gardening messes
and cluttered storage,
proclamations of power and independence
and withdrawal forever

(such a long time)
I perceive insanity's repetition
(downward to darkness
on extended wings)
nibbling at edges of peripheral vision
I imagine some x-files
alien black oil seeping
through my eyeballs, nostrils
tonsils alive with unknown bacteria
is there no drug?
no safe-free-of-side-effects
drug to protect from
acid venomous
words, paralyzing
varnish vapor words
like stupid always never useless
the wounded fearful cornered words
wind driven lashings of sleet words
(wide water without sound,
I think, why should I give
my bounty to the dead?
today I find no comforts
of the sun, no divinity
within myself)
but Jason needs an answer:
I flush yeast and Rid-X once a month.
Thank you he says
click; even the telemarketer
has the last word
(a dividing and indifferent blue)

Cumberland Head Moment: Early Morning Run

Full moon-set: I, modern mythical heroine
Goddess empowered, sprint easterly
Along tide-sculpted Northern shore ridge
Blue black slate, granite boulders,
Intricate cedar limbs, resourceful survivors
These wild faces, mimicked by water spirits
And a clan of Canadian geese
(By my right hand)
My perfect shadow, vibrant
High on still water surface,
Cast
    As
Red sun erupts, spills morning's lava-light
Onto earth corn forests, golden-baled hay cylinders
(By my left hand)
My broad dream-strides pace
The soaring seagulls' source
Above heat currents
Uplifted
    As
My perfect shadow, vivid black
Rises higher still on water surface
Legs stretch, arms swing
In motion, balance, harmony
With pink cloud backdrop
Child, sister, mother, god
Minute atom, the universe:
I am the moment.

Decision

A man I loved
Before I could fly
Said to me
Atop a misty mountain,
Leaning philosophically
On ski poles,
That a racoon in a trap
Will chew off its own leg
To free itself.
I reflected a moment
On the analogy
And began to
Shiver in fresh wind,
Anxious to slide
Down the mountain
Below the clouds
To see wide vistas.
As clouds raced by then
Seeking new scenes
And shelter from North winds,
I sought to shape
My reply;
Fingers chilled, knees stiffening,
I prepared to speak.
This man I loved
Leaned forward intently
My smile hinting a joke
But believe me
I meant it:
Far better to limp
Through life's dangers
absent a leg than meet
Death by freezing.
Yet fast limping exhausts;
traps remembered seem
somehow settled, secure.

DOPAMINE AND PERIWINKLE

Advice to the artist this morning:
Engage, engage in your work
To keep the dopamine flowing
Prevent catatonia, lethargy, or
Writers block; thus, to avoid
Distracting myself again, annoyed
With too many flying hops
superfluous road trips there
And shopping binge stare
more political despair,
meddling in other peoples' affairs,
now build momentum
For that huge leap of faith
determination to
Finish my project this year
No matter what, no matter what
Up the slope, I'll write now
A running poem replete with
Forward Motion and Technicolor,
Stimulate production in
That center that produces
Dopamine, I'll think of
Periwinkle, my favorite color
Splashed across a huge canvas
Just too much of it, she says,
too much, awash in periwinkle frenzy,
It spills over the sides
And up the walls,
Periwinkle out the windows,
Periwinkle uplift in the sky,
Swooping under the sea,
Pale periwinkle dancing in the
Clouds at horizon's edge,
Deep periwinkle soaring

above the bridge where
My little plane floats upwind,
miming the awesome pelican,
"whose beak can hold more
than his belly-can" childhood's rhyme,
Across the barrier islands
So much, so much abundance,
A profusion of periwinkle,
beside white sand ribbons,
Left rudder right aileron
Into crosswind, crab-slip:
Altitude is your friend but
So too the ground.
Clear to land, runway 4,
Ah, there it is! A poem more.

September 11, 2017

Sixteen years, it's been.
A stick outside, mailed from
The National Arbor Foundation
two years ago is now a sturdy maple
seven feet high; last night, the eye
or what remained of Hurricane Irma's
eye, passed overhead, my granddaughter
asleep in the bedroom next door.
Odd that we made no mention of
that other catastrophe.
She was not yet three that day.
We speak of uncertainty,
vague, unspeakable dread,
terror of the unknown
as though none before us, none
elsewhere, shares experience
so devastating as our own.

In the morning, powerless,
bending, stretching, reaching, breathing,
Florida humid unconditioned air,
I recall my Shanghai students,
after morning Tai Chi,
dancing and singing lyrics we practiced,
State TV filming,
videotapes distributed, (for classroom use)
glorious intercultural exchange
(and copyright infringement)
yet the chorus of Chinese teachers
ready to spark their young Chinese students
swaying to "It's the CIRCLE OF LIFE!"
and "He LIVES IN YOU", Lion King
highlights, such joy and fellowship
erupted, laughter, language and love,

we shared our universals,
our cultural revolution horrors,
our fear of reprisals for openness, forgotten,
Our governments irrelevant,
celebrants of humanity, summer 2001.

But Towers fell. Borders closed. SARS spewed.
Wars grew.

Impossible years later, I read
the Lion's "Circle of Life" continues:
Disney English Schools
across China now, and
perhaps I'm partly responsible
for that; at least I
didn't leak state weapons
secrets. Or maybe
these were.
At least I didn't give
uranium.
To those who despise
the Disney-fied
I apologize.

CRUISE ADJUST

Humanitarian

Give money sometimes to Amnesty International and Save the Children and a
Few other good causes but I'm not Mother Teresa or anything
And my job, you know, I'm always trying to pump up the kids,
Get 'em interested in something outside of here
Outside of them and I get so intense going on and on
About Bosnia and Rwanda and Ethiopia and Sudan one day
And ethnic cleansing and we gotta care about others and
So something and it all starts with your heart, one person
Look at Nelson Mandela in prison 27 years and he became
President apartheid over, the power of one, you know?
And then this girl in the front row gets up, the front row mind you
Right in front of my eyes
And she's crying and she waves a pass in my face says she's leaving
For the funeral and it's like a bomb hits me or lightning or
Whatever stunning cliché you wan
What funeral I say
My grandma she was my best friend
Lived with us all my life and she's gone now
How can I go on? And I give her this big hug
And I'm humble and feeling dumb now
Cause I hadn't even noticed the pain
In my own classroom
In the front row, mind you
Right in front of my eyes
Great humanitarian
On a soap box
Humanitarian

Photograph of the Ancestress

Strong, hard, but single-minded she was,
Dissipated dreams of intrepid conestoga
Journeys west
Turned vision and strength to bitter
Tight-lipped anger,
The boredom and drudgery of routine and
Repetition wrought silent vengeance
Upon daughters who yearned, too
For adventure.

No velvet glove softened the rule
Of her iron fist,
No frivolous lace bordered her
Daughters' dark frocks.
Serious discipline crushed struggles against
Her regulation,
Their laughter faded quickly with
Their fantasies, frozen
sepia-stern as the jaw
of the ancestress.

Sepia can't hide the rest,
that fury, thirst, longing:
what did such resentment build?
My mother told me stories.
One daughter became a surgeon;
another ran a ranch. A third faced an asylum
on returning, shamed and poor, from
elopement to Africa, her mysterious madness
still a matter of opinion, but her music survives.
They never
considered acting in Hollywood.
Results are more than a mere
hashtag me too
and lawsuits, but
no one sees progress
from sepia;
it is just a format
photo option.

Supplicant

October's colorful promise gone,
The tree outside the classroom window listens

to her rasp, "Look in the dictionary
and check each word for spelling!"

My neighbor's class an agonizing
exercise in authority, dominance

And submission.
"Are you saying you don't even have a pencil?"

The naked tree listens uncomfortably;
outside, it squirms arthritic November

limbs painfully skyward,
supplicants for mercy:

What is the harm in telling him how to spell it?
Giving a pencil?

She missed the story that child wanted to tell.
He's forgotten it, now.

The tree's prayer is answered:
The bell rings.

WHITEOUT

Teacher, got any white-out?

Wrenched from black on blinding white daydream
of Saturday's January illusion,

late afternoon out on the ice, my long black shadow
etched on crisp sculpted snowdrifts,

sharp, like pen and India ink,
filled in, on deathbed white paper:

A shock!

I'd forgotten, for years,
I had a shadow.

Looking back, I thought I'd
turn to white pillar salt

Not for one last glimpse
No not punishment

Not lack of faith, no not that
but from all those

waves of salt tears turned
crusty, shriveled, fossilized.

Wind gust snow white-out.
Teacher, got any white-out?

Sloppy white corrections
of imperfect black.

Exorcism – Student Poet and Standardized Tests

With both hands
you handed me
your poems, carefully
tied with yellow ribbons
your eyes cast down insecurely
hope veiled by eyelids
hooded, half dreaming
of applause, half fearing
ridicule,
but the bell rang,
and I had to move
to another class,
stacked with piles of
pre-test essays to read
and respond not edit with
my vicious new teacher
red pen, carving
Injurious marks, scars, across
Emergent expression, struggling sentences.
By the time I rescued
your collection
of despairing poems
sandwiched among
seven crammed class folders,
hundreds to be "tested", standardized:
you, the miracle,
had dropped out
of school,
your family had
"relocated"
all this
in one vacation week;
perhaps that's
how poets are born
or how they die.

Teaching Sonnets (with thanks to #29 William Shakespeare)

When sometimes classes seem to bring me down
And I self-centered, will bemoan my state
Quite sure that students see my vacant frown
Demanding more than time allows one to create,
Wishing they were geniuses and I the mentor
Applause from distant hands in my mind's eye
The cheers of those who make of me the center
With choruses of praise from those on high,
Right then self- loathing brings me to reality
And joy for those around me I can feel
(Like running 'long the beach, the pelicans rising
To heights of freedom) my heart's true zeal,
It's then I realize such gratitude,
My strength comes from this very soul food.

Inspiration and Censors: Monumental Adventure of the Turds

Ken, working on his puppet show script
Quietly scribbling and drawing,

Marvelous engagement, absorbed in his task
The teacher's dream for all.

But for emotionally disturbed Ken,
A miracle each day

I slide by his desk to glimpse over
His shoulder:

"The Monumental Adventure of the Turds."
Tactfully I try to suggest losing the title;

my fear of parents overwhelms.
Perhaps "reinvent" the title?

I purse my lips, evidence of command,
and he says ok compliantly; I move on to

others, confident in my success, wisdom
and guidance. Gliding by again some time

later, I'm riveted to the new title: "The Monumental
Adventure of the Feces."

Excrement, I think, might fool would-be censors,
but my fear requires boundaries:

In my frustration, I say impatiently, "OK,

I'm sick of this *crap*," and before

the words have left my mouth
I hear too late the mistaken pun,

and further inspiration
escapes me.

Fahrenheit 451 Poem

Dear Montag:
If you dream of flames
choking thought, masking
memory, and
ashes of charred flesh
up your nostrils,
feathered butterfly pages
searing your cheeks
and hollow laughter
echoing down empty
wells, down, down
Never-quite-touching-
Bottom-no-never-
quite-touching-
anything
sheltered from opposing thought
free of offensive ideas,
protected in safe spaces
spinning on snapchat or
Facebook or CNN chatter
meaningless micro-aggression repetition
Instagram simple
consumer consumed
it means you have died
been born again
a child of the new universe
free of that centrifuge
whirling society to
pieces, you are
free
to build
again.

Dead Poets Society

They hunch over paper
writing by candlelight
held in its flicker,
the world smaller, close,
intimate for a moment.
The scolding teacher
next door doesn't shake this
chance to dive into the
shipwreck and salvage an
odd treasure, a sliver of silver,
perhaps a shard of antique gold,
some shred of old clothing from
a sealed trunk,
something lost
long, long ago.
Or something from
under the bed,
or at the far closet corner,
the kitchen floor before,
pictures in scrapbooks.
I sneak a glance at
the teenage girl who wrote last week,
"I remember when my mother's
boyfriend kicked my dog
with his steel-toed boots,
again and again.
Sparky's yelping howl of pain
filled the universe,
and he limped off the porch,
into the road, blind with agony,
and was hit by a car.
I'm glad he died quickly.
This is no world for a good dog
To live in."
She's smiling, now.
Mercifully, she remembers
something else
today.

Destination in Sight
Shanghai Teaching First Year

1
Senior teacher Zhou's smile-mask
Slipped a moment
When asked why
The Great Memorial to the Martyrs
Mentioned Mao but once

Solo visitor, intrepid female teacher
From America, I approach
that statuary guarding eighth- wonder pyramid
the massive movement in marble

Too alive for sculpture,
tortured men, women with sick babies
Roll, reach forward, upward to
Stand tall, chains broken

Impossible to stroll past,
Without halting, paying homage,
Without the urge to bow or pray
In thick punishing heat, scalding sun

Inside, dark cold blast, stilted military
Cast of solemn silent guides gesture
The way, each follows close,
Arms rigid at sides until
Quick seize of my uplifted camera, mei wenti, dui bu qi so sorry

the mixed media raises questions,
the awe of young faces
martyrs of Shanghai,
haunt the black marble wall.
Down, down, icy still air
Catacomb walk, torch lit,

My footsteps echo, ghosts escort,
my guards vanish, why?
I approach the prison, alone, an embarrassed shivering
solitary imperialist

Zhou's answer later (he would not go): Not everything
Mao did was good.
We try to remember
Some good, some bad.
We move toward future
Xu Ping's answer:
We do not
Discuss such things.

2
After the woman feeds us
Hand- made jiaozi, xifan with
Pickled vegetables, wonton
In broth, impossible breakfast
Thank you. Xie xie.
Monday's ride to work
Through science fiction
Cityscape, architecture
Of skyscrapers and cranes
In motion (cranes the
National bird, tired joke)
Superstructures, traditional pagodas hinted
in twenty story glass and steel, block by block
the hovels razed,
resurrected further west.

In secret Zhou confides:
I was taken from university,
Sent to work in labor camp
In countryside.
Four years. It was nightmare.
They took my father, a doctor,

To farm.
His eyes harden, go away
A moment.
Suddenly, he smiles lightly, says:
I was weak, but I became
Strong. Have more shrimp.
Their color is celebration.

3
Beijing:
Squeezed, herded on line, squares
With Tens of thousands
Filing past Mao's body,
Many weeping.
(Great famous photograph
At Tiennamen's end
Burns on retina
Superimposed tanks,
Bloodshed in my mind's eye.)

But Quandung Province child
Purchases plastic flowers
For me, will not accept payment,
A gift,
she says shyly,
Practicing halting English
to make her
"Richer in
different way"
Asks me
to take her picture
Instead.
Remember me.
I am WuXie.
Translation:
I am
A speck on an overcrowded

Troubled planet. Still
Remember me.

back "home" from Beijing
Shanghai hotel staff
Gather in karaoke room
Singing cultural revolution songs,
Like we sing Beatles, or CCR
Or Rolling Stones
Weeping, dancing, Laughing, drinking
Chrysanthemum tea
To keep cool,
Or beer to forget
The neighborhood communist party
Office on the opposite side
Of the parking lot
Is closed until
Daylight.
They relive with us their
Tumultous teenage years.
We hug, dance together,
Know spy planes are
diplomacy postures:
Childish, silly, empty

4
Travel outside Shanghai
Only creates a longing to return.
Even Venice-like garden Suzchou is staged,
Like Tong Li, Like Hangchou's Amusement park, like
Hutong District Beijing, All Disney-fied.
But Shanghai is real,
As real as temple incense
And piled grapes the size of plums
Secular blessings upon
The sacred world,
Sacred blessing

Of the mundane.
People dance classical ballroom
On the street nights, urge us to join in;
Steamy heat forces cooking outdoors
Onto the sidewalks, on overpasses,
Whole families cook delicious concoctions,
Play mahjong,
Hold the babies with
Slits in pants over
The curb, no landfill nightmares here
not disposable, bio degrades

Ubiquitous bamboo scaffolding, tough as steel,
Constant motion, rivers of commuters on bikes
White gloved ladies, child and briefcase behind
Stop at the red- light dam, all ignore
23rd century subway, gleaming with glass;
lanes of hovel life teem behind
gated complexes:
the tinted glass mercedes
hides whoever it is
honking for bicycles to scatter;
still, on the sidewalk, ni hao smiles
mei wenti, dui bu qi
xie, xie:
hello, very good, I'm sorry, thank you

5
Students present me roses
One at a time
They sing a song I taught them
As farewell,
Chinese Bette Midlers:
"Just remember
in the winter
far beneath the bitter snow
lies zda seed zdat with the

sun's rove, in zda spring
becomes the rose.

Classroom "show and tell"
Became the confessional
Not forced,
But earnest confessional habit

Memorized English phrases like:
"China is very open now
China wants peace with America
We do not discuss Chinese politics"

Slipped away, like Zhou's smile-mask.

Tell us about your Christmas Festival, they begged.
They shared their mother-in-law stories
Wishes for children, and longing
For nature, for clean air.
Shanghai teachers sang,
became the springtime roses
emerging from beneath
bitter snow.

Classics

They smashed his violin,
forced him to work heavy labor
saying he might not feel so superior;
Half century later, the old
Chinese maestro plays Mozart
with his eight- year- old granddaughter
on the corner of a busy south Chicago
intersection, for donations, for free,
for love.
He'd be safer outside
this gun-free zone, of course,
some place that might protect him
if attacked by jealous racists;
down the street, they dump red paint
on a statue of Lincoln, and tear down
whatever they can't pawn.
He's never taken a nickel of government
money, and now his subversive music
flows into the hood:
Mozart softens frantic city noise
Like a cultural revolution.

Covering Bases

"So superstitious, los indigenos,"
my Guatemalan mother would mutter
in disgust, each morning,
when the servant tossed pinches
of corn flour in the four directions,
"Ah, this Quiche culture so strange,"
retiring to her room for study
of her civilized catechism
on the miracles of the Virgin.
Later that week, after classes,
exploring the outskirts,
high on a mountaintop,
led by a small wide-grinned boy in rags,
I witnessed a wedding ceremony, secret,
A young Quiche couple kneeling
before artfully piled stone altar
amidst smoke and incense,
to protect from evil, mingle their spirits
with songs of birds, ancestors;
ancient winds,
whispered chants drifted
toward my discreet path viewpoint,
near old supervising grandmother, working her
magic loom, quetzals, parrots, purple-pink-orange-blue
green-red-aqua designs shaped,
colored by collective archetypal memory,
local organic dyes.

"Mañana, el padre y l'iglesia," she
confided quietly in halting Spanish, her
second language. Tomorrow the priest
and the church. "Pero la mayor part es hoy:
Ellos hacen el amor," she smiled timidly.
But the most important part is today.
They make love.

Melting - Renga Form - Seasons

Squadron of snow geese honking
Finally returning
V's North

Snow and sleet beat
Windowbox daffodils
They remain steadfast, brave

Ancient Haitian woman lugs groceries up subway stairs
Pussywillows peek from the bag
The cab driver grumbles

Rocking side to side, the train soothes
Lakes and mountains race by

Moonscape, snowscape
Valleys awash in light
Mountains crouch protectively

Longing for the chairs
By the fireplace
Holding hands

When a north country man loves you
There's dry, seasoned wood
Cut, split and stacked in cords

Garden tools in the shed
Lean against the back wall

The dog waits patiently
Hoping for table scraps
Sighs heavily to remind us

Monday is garbage day

Truck is early this time

Abandoned baseball cap
Nostalgia's whispers
Of summer games, youth

Sailboat's captain races round the mark
The rush of fulfillment

Watching peach-pink sunset together
No two alike
Another precious day

The last leaves drift earthward
Our first hike together

Harvest moon eclipses mall
Seems a space ship
Huge and alien

Woodstove smoke
Blankets the valley
Overripe apples scent the cold air

Coffee grounds and fruit peels
Make excellent compost
Health food for plants

Tofu will never
Replace meat

I am more hungry
For spring tulips
Than even spaghetti

Yesterday I saw
Tiny green shoots
Reach through the thawing earth

STORMS ALTER COURSE

Alphabets of Fear

abandoned, breathless
Breaking barriers, carries dread
Efficiently, furiously
Forward; gusty, harrowing, it just kicks
Little moments noticed or provoked;
Queer remembrances start tumbling
Underground, veiled warnings, wailings,
X-ray you zealously.
Abandoned again
Broken colossus,
Deadly efficient ego, freakish
Gargantuan holocaust iteration
Jars kaleidoscopic lightning,
Monuments nulled, odious
Pariahs quench restive searching
Tides' undercurrent vast water,
Xenophobic yells Zero-hour!

Pulling the Plug

I read: "*Her only daughter was with her when she died.*"
The others so noble in sacred death, experiencing the moment
    "*when the soul moves toward the light
    the gentle fulfillment of life's cycle.*"
In fury, hideous guilt
I seize the torment, blue black bruises
misshapen gnarled shadows hover
gleaming needles shine, plastic tubes drip
something pretending life
machinery beeping rigidly rhythmic robotic
a nurse's confusion
over my tardiness, her wishes,
my brother's stone face,
my desperate departure.

Bye, mom. I see you didn't wait.
I love you mom.
(She wasn't there.)

Much easier to talk to her now
These many years later
She talks back
almost.
I couldn't wait for that moment
when the electricity stopped
moving blood, air pumps

in the end
Mother's face
didn't look

felt only (transparent blue thin membrane)
    Skin
and (brittle, shriveled, dry sea shell)

    Bones
saw (needle seepage dried orange blood, blue veined ruined skeleton)
    Hands
heard (whirring, pumping, rhythmic, dead)
    Machines
smelled/tasted (stale medicines, acidic hamburger, rancid onion husks)
Nothing.

Remembering Skippy Neushaffer

You'd have been surprised
If you'd been there.
He's forty- eight,
Pretty tough guy.
Not a stone, no, he's got a heart
But with those temper tantrums
You sometimes forget
And things have to be just so,
You know? No surprises, not even
A birthday party or holiday, just
No surprises please.
You'd have been surprised
If you'd been there
To hear him speak, and break down
In tears, quietly, finally.
He'd deny it, of course, the tears,
But I was there, sitting in
A fourthfloor café in Montreal
Those forty something years later
Listening to him tell about
Skippy Neushaffer.

Hard to see this tough guy a child
But we all were, weren't we?
And there he was, not only a child of
An angry, bitter father,
But a sickly child, who needed
Months at Columbia Presbyterian
Hospital, months at a time,
months alone, mostly, with
parents a state away, working-
months with a changing cast of
characters as aides, nurses, doctors,
other children in a dormitory setting;

but one, just one, was there
for a long, long time, and this one
became a friend because he had the same
catheter and the same urine bag
and liked to play "go fish" and "rummy"
and his parents came every day because
they lived close by and greeted both little boys
with gusto and playfulness.
The Neushaffers were the
light of his days.

And this tough guy tells me
he saw a child yesterday, reminded
him of Skippy Neushaffer,
a five- year- old with a crew-cut
and big blue eyes, playful
parents beside him. "Here I am
forty something years later," he says,
"and I'm thinking about Skippy Neushaffer.
Imagine that," he says. "I don't
Understand why."

"One night, after months in
the hospital together, Skippy woke me
up in the middle of the night.
He said, 'Tommy, I have to go now.'
'Okay. I'll really miss you.'
He didn't say anything more.
I went to sleep.
When I woke up, daylight,
his bed was empty. Through
some mix-up in communication,
his parents came
into the room, saw the empty bed,
and cried out, 'Oh, my God, Skippy!'
They never even looked over at me."

I mean to say, but don't, tell me about how the nurses
explained, tell me how your mother comforted,
tell me how you were counseled through
the loss of your friend, tell me what
you feel about it now, tell me
how I can help. Tell me what his
parents said to you, "tell me. . . ."

"It was the fifties," he says.
"People didn't worry about
That touchy-feely shit.
He was gone, and I had to
go through the next few surgeries
and recoveries without him.
I lived, he didn't make it.
I got over it. Just thought about him
is all. Who decides which of us
makes it, which of us doesn't?
Funny, but all these years later,
I think of him, and. . .and. . . . I don't know. . ."

I saw the tears, I did.
He'll deny them.
Took a long time, but they came.

This message is for you, Skippy,
you treasured soul,

from a grateful stranger
on this craggy rock
turning in black space
amidst all the star billions,

ubiquitous, unique

Pro-Choice: Fifty-One

"After all the warnings, the fears, a woman's mistakes are different from a girl's, they are fire on stone, they are a trait not an error." Janet Fitch, White Oleander

I awoke in a bath of fear
White chrome light
scalds moonscape on retina,
long needles twisting, turning
inside me.
Worse than death,
lost in whispers, high pitched
machines whining in
timeless monotony.

Alone or not? Confusion
Void, above, a searing
white light circle
then black. The end, if so
the end of what? If there is loss,
then loss of what? Peripheral
questions, I need to know.
But I am dreaming, and
yet here by choice, no
answers. The laughter
isn't friendly. I reach with my mind to
touch something, or cradle. My arms will not
move. No longer mine.
White blood pumps furiously
Somewhere. I listen for breathing,
A sign that all is as it was.
I hear nothing.

Fifty-One

          Fifty-One: The Movie Trailer Remake
        "Ask any woman how old he'd be now. She'll know."
                -Barbara Kingsolver, *Animal Dreams*

Who could imagine then,
With years stretched ahead, the choices made
Seemed almost trivial compared to rich potential
Of material, the experience, the coming events trailers,
Our lives a grand epic for which the minor characters, virtually
Unknowns, didn't have a voice.
The music soundtrack was symphonic, broad and sweeping, wild and
harmonic, choral.
No solo undercurrent's message sent; I couldn't hear the piccolo
Then.

We had no pictures, no sound, no little voice
it was not for lack of caring or salient information, but rather
A belief that
unheard drumbeats
made possible the unthinkable
Then.

There was music.
I had some wine. Blood flowed, I sobbed. Trumpets of victory, violins for sins
It was all my fault. I thought I knew about death
Then.

Ever since, I've changed my mind, and though I'd not fight another
Deny her chance, I know I could not again,
Myself, live in that dead place more. Yesterday, my daughter
Lost a still small voice,
twelve weeks in utero,
the picture vivid,

Before our eyes, the heartbeat stopped, hormone numbers dropped.
Gazing at the ultrasound, our agony within,
She wanted more than anything
for a chance I gave up
Then.

ORATORIO SOCIETY RECOVERED

We shared our copy of Messiah.
I sang soprano, she sang alto.
We practiced all Autumn
for the community choir.
I was eleven, just menstrual.
Soon enough, a daughter saw
mother shrink to fit father;
once tall, slim, regal and witty
well- traveled, well storied, musical,
she began her decline, binding feet
with flat shoes, hunched posture.
Once wise wolf woman, wildly whimsical, she slouched, paws crippled,
howl muted, music withheld,
welled beneath her skin,
fermented, turned acid, bitter, corrosive,
beneath torrents of his drunken invective, endless ball game static
like maddening Geiger counter self-doubt,
holidays swept away by
jealous tornadoes, schemes screamed;
she had thought to soften this
fatherless father with redemptive religion,
her prescription for his angry self-loathing.
Misguided faith delayed too long
the day she escaped, trading
one slavery for alcohol's lash.
Years later, I approved disconnection of hospital wires, gray tubes,
ghastly chrome digital meters, added my hollow, whispered
apologies to brain-dead ears of
the skeleton phantom, said goodbye
in a stupor, gazing insensate at the shriveled facsimile of myself.
Deus ex machina: my many mothers
nurtured me, reconciled the wreckage, survivors' songs the sirens'
strains, melody and counterpoint,
harmony over dissonance, rhythm amidst chaos,
until I could sing with her again.
Mother sings here now
in this Oratorio Society.

ADJUST FLIGHT

Brass Quintet and Choir at Epiphany, St. Mary's in St. Petersburg: Gratitude

Nourishing friend, explores my hunger for chorus, offers

an afternoon concert together away from football playoffs

Promise of gelato to follow, here, an international waterfront city.

Alleluia in vast voices and keys, registers and modulations,

spanning centuries in St. Mary's acoustics, breathtaking echoes,

designed to convert us,
genius skills interpreted

by gifted descendants, disciplined practice

to Inspire! In spiritu,
breathe in holy love, exhale joy

Allegro molto ritmico, maestoso;
adagio, and allegro this sinfonia sacra,
Alleluia, alleluia, yes, let men their songs employ, let every heart prepare
room, yes, praise and glory,
Accept the offering, yes, we faithful come to sing
Joy to the world, with drums and cymbals, psalms and arias, yes

To rejoice with angels,
the divinity in our midst.
Alleluia, yes
birth of newborn
peace, yes

Picasso meets Pachelbel on Perico's Bayou: a tribute to Cindy after "jamming"

Plays Prokofiev-Stravinsky piano with passion,
Then shifts to chords' more melodic fashion,
bad cop good cop, blue devil angel
Cubed conflict cultural, northeast canon changed,
Planted now at bayou's edge
beside her treasured piano pledged
Guitar strings hum her new compositions
Lyrics utter life's re-definitions
All dissonance now strengthens absolution
As syncopated rhythms seek resolution
The fourth, the fifth, the seventh added
Tension dissolves with soul's tonic triad.
Her piece entitled "Frankenstein
At the Renaissance Fair?" soulfully sinfully
Super sublime.

Maro's Art Show: Beyond to Destinations Unknown (Ekphrastic)

Where to place the horizon?
Indeed, that is life's challenge,
Whether to accept boundaries
Self-described, or prescribed by others,
Whether to dream and long for more
Or remember paradise within,
The joys of macro, micro:
Cosmic, interstellar journey,
Or minute, unique reverie,
Transcendent "now"?

Oh yes. Where is the horizon?
Have I covered this ground already?
Did this sandy path lagoon heal,
or this sea scene sensation
happen in this life in this jungle?
Are those mountains against
Retina's backdrop waters
my history, my present gift, or
my future?

Am I to relearn lessons I forgot?
And where to place regret and loss,
Or hope and innocence
Amidst these flying spirits?
Upon wings, or beneath them,
the wings themselves, or the
source that guides wings?
I remember soaring.
The wind.
How close here am I to "there"?

At this moment, right now,
Where my feet are?

Craving the distant is human,
while too seeking capture, possession,
each moment's experience,
perhaps carry beyond the horizon
destination unknown.

Jars Poetica (with a tongue in cheek thanks to Archibald Macliesh, "Ars Poetica")

A jar should be nostalgic
Like a home-canned aspic

Clothed in gingham
Like homemade jam

Silently telling a story
Without those details gory

Suggesting a hope, to feel
solace of a shared meal

A jar should wait in the cupboard dark
For discovery by creative spark

Releasing, as garlic sautéed in olive oil,
Memories of feasts and kitchen toil

Releasing salivary glands
with tastes of cumin, masala, other lands

A jar should rest in the cupboard dark
For discovery by creative spark

A jar should represent the thought
Not preach ought

For all the world's chaos, pain and strife
Suggest peanut butter, jelly, white bread, a knife.

For love:
Homemade chicken broth and noodles

A jar should not define
Just offer.

PRE-LANDING CHECKLIST

Millibars

Something in the familiar red yellow green mass
on my computer screen, cycling
counter my clock toward the blue dot, me
centered by millibars a recognition,
a re cog while he explained
painstakingly, the offshore buoy system,
wave heights and barometers, some
unfunded now,
and we laughed again
over the notion of man-made hurricanes
the centric of ego, the cycle of cog,
the re of everything.
My dream once more counter of
climate, my blue dot blinking
feebly as power fails:
I've traded my candles
this hurricane
for a generator,
a millibar here,
another down,
Something familiar in the big pots of chili,
scrambling to reaffirm that blue dot, me
centered by pixeled masses
spinning up the coast,
inland to fresh dirt,
higher ground
my dream blinks
off and on
cumin, coriander, chopped tomatoes
garlic and red beans
off, on blue blink
pulse

How it Works Sometimes

Setting: Just after the central Florida railroad tracks,
6 or 7 trains a night, at least,
past tiny, algae covered Lake Lillian
and that patch of cows
before the cement truck cemetery,
this rural town where you could pass seven storefront-small churches
with thrift shops in a half mile of country roads,
one proclaims under the heading, "Ramah Baptist Church"
"Free HIV Testing.",
across the road from a huge billboard
which warns: "Only cowards kill animals."
Plot and Characters: The pretty girl in the Subway t shirt
came to the AA meeting sullen and quiet;
from behind rotten teeth she covered
with the backs of her small hands, growled quietly
when pushed by the old timers to identify herself,
"I'm just here to do my time. I got into some trouble New Year's Eve and
I'm just here to do my time and pay my bills and keep to myself that's
all I want.
Don't need nothing from nobody. Stay outta trouble, that's all I want."
An aged marine responded with the tradition, "Keep Coming Back", and
then unbelievably told about his couples massage with his wife for their
60th wedding anniversary over at New Smyrna Beach. Sober.
His buddy derided him unmercifully when the Marine also admitted to
a pedicure.
Conflict: Finally, Maggie, a sweet old lady, tidy white hair, smiling
Through piercing blue eyes, drawled,
"If ya want help stayin' way from a drink
One day at a time, see me after
what these bozos are calling a meeting.
Resolution: Reluctantly, the girl reached for the telephone number, used it

Denouement: The dentist in the group did the young girl's teeth
over six months for free, the lawyer

got her a suspended sentence, the hairdresser
did a makeover; Maggie and Mary
helped her see some sunlight
without a drink
our #metoo: "alcohol gave us wings to fly, but took away our sky";
you wouldn't recognize her now,
her arm around a shaking newbie clutching
fresh DUI papers to sign

Answering a Student Email:
or
Excuse Me, I'm Going to Fly My Airplane Now

I realize you misunderstand my caution
to *save all drafts*
and *notes* in case you might need
to *use ideas* again;
your *"writer's notebook"* meant one thing to me
and another to you.
To me, scribbled notes and lists,
outlines, brainstorms, short writes, doodles
offer a treasure trove
of inspiration and short stories, essays, poems
and found literature.
To you, they are clutter and baggage,
weight to carry from car to class,
retrieved from grocery lists and cans,
Taco Bell wrappers and under- seat umbrellas,
appeasement, hopes an essay emerges with a letter grade.

My guidance was intended to nurture nascent ideas,
(*Look up the word*)
to bless emergent spring semester efforts,
but instead I trampled upon your time
and sense of organization.
What do *you* think? (About anything? No, strike that.)

Your essay should have a thesis, a claim of policy, value,
or fact supported by evidence (from your life, your ideas, your examples,
maybe even *from your Writer's Notebook responses* to things we've read
and discussed. . .oh, wait, your attendance has been poor. . .)

It should be fresh, focused with a noticeable pattern of organization, using precise language and varied sentence structure, blah blah.
If you insist on word count, try 750-1000.
Please: no ending cliché like "Now I know I must live each day to the fullest."
Even if it's as true as it ever was. (*Dependent clause*)
I'd rather be writing something else.

The short answer is this:
no, you can't submit the same essay twice and have it count for two.

Disney and Dali Exhibit
St. Petersburg, Florida

In the sepia photo, they seemed almost
forbidden lovers
two small town boys with wildness,
bridled imaginations which must merge, must

be perhaps one day *un*bridled

A failed project, a film called "Destino"
Dali craved making
with his fellow genius, ironically
titled in light of its outcome,
but the drawings, the false starts and restarts,
the resurrection of prior concepts, the process,
try again, dive underwater, then fly, then become
song, first one bell then the butterfly then goddess

grace and form, mud's metamorphosis
become the other. But the goddess will sue.

I see my own trap there, know
my poems unpublishable,
those published a few
years back, a mistake I see now,
an editor thought I was black
her congratulatory call faltered when she
heard me speak.

For others, I spoke, became the other:
Point of view a "no-no", now.
Publishers frown, hire "appropriateness"
editors, empathy is
"Cultural appropriation",

Or worse. Imagination regulations.
Exceptions for white privilege tenured, though.

Dali's drawings were hidden. I imagine piles and stacks
of folders, scraps and sketches, and see my own
space, ever larger, ever smaller, makes no difference.
Partners make no difference. With, without.
Distractions abound. I make them, those frenzied
joys, those delights of experience.
Despair of discipline.
'Shoulds' abound.

Disney loved Dali's ideas, but despaired of product.

After all, Disney built empire. Finished. Completed.
Focused. Sacrificed.

The two duel forever within:

The timepiece draped in a desert

challenged by a talking mouse

in a vast magic kingdom.

Memories are the Pillows of Life: AGP

My brother collected wise sayings, called them,
"Ancient Gaelic Proverbs."
This one on memories stirs more than most,
my associations with pillows, the ghosts:

together, when I was 6, he 10, we packed candy filled
pillowcases onto bicycles,
we ran away from home,
the fights we fled not pillow fights,
but alcohol's psycho warfare

pillow cases in laundry, blood spattered,
our journey was hope through neighborhood forests
we pedaled furiously, sure to escape the dis ease
resolved to recover, moving forward, milky way
fortified, Snickers strengthened, distant shouts
wisps of spring wind, immune to destiny

No casket pillows beneath my own deceased loved ones' heads:
cremated all, haunting always,
and here this tactile pink sticky note,
written in my brother's hand, beautiful, artistic,
(like my mother's hand)
beside a picture of his boys laughing
on my sailboat decades ago;

guilt crawls wormlike
through my decaying psyche
others' loved ones arranged in funerals as
embalmed dolls resting peacefully on pink satin,
reminding me that as in everything else, I took
what I thought was the easier path,

dispensing ashes, brother and father together,
from the Road Not Taken deck in Tampa Bay,
sprinkled upon the aqua altar, frigate birds soaring:
First, the Navy Hymn (solemn), for my father was
a Pacific War hero on destroyers

Next, "The Parting Glass" (Irish tears), "they're sorry for my goin' away,"
dancing Irish jigs (Connachtman, I think),
then
homage to our times with Clancy Brothers

before my head finally rested, cradled

in humid night cairn

upon memories.

BETWEEN

the space occupying before

and after

two items in today's reading:

a poem by Nicole Callihan,
Oklahoma girl gone Brooklyn/NYU
explores that space of infusion, joy, terror
when first she heard in spring,
"Music of the Night" in headphones
clamped onto her ears by a boy

everything now possible

and

Laisa Souza, Brazilian aerial skier, gymnast,
motion and rhythm, sensation and soaring
stopped cold by a tree on a black diamond trail
in Park City, Utah, rescue helicopter blades roar.
Now wheelchair bound girl dreams
maybe someday to touch her hand
to her face just once,
asks God what new task is
required of her each day when

everything seems impossible

yes, I am in the space

between these two

perhaps something is possible

there

DOWNWIND AND SLOW FLIGHT

Cessna Altitude Clock

a gift pays tribute to our flying hobby, nestled in

its prime Eastern-facing shelf,

the first to greet

the sunrise each morning.
across the top, the word, "altitude."

Just awake from

dark, restless dreams, wherein I'm a member of
some symphony
performing by the sea,

anxious where I'll rest my head at night,
once the flute is put back in its case.

With my fresh coffee, I pause, seek guidance,
meditate some,

and at about eight before eight, the big hand
completely covered the "L";

the sun poured in like Joni Mitchell's butterscotch,
and I wondered whether it was the caffeine,

or my higher power, that made me laugh

out loud

YOGA PRACTICE WITH CUSTOMER SERVICE

Long breaths, stretching open the heart, lifting forward
The love, the best intention, patience,
Exhaling slowly like blowing fog on a mirror
She says, (the yoga teacher that is,
Not the customer service representative.)

please hold, our computers are slow today,
Please wait while I transfer you to someone
Who will check your file.

My third transfer, but isn't life
Just one transfer after another?

Pay attention to your breath,
Straighten your back to clear the power
Connecting earth to sky, feel your
Feet on the cold tile, stretch your toes,

no record of your other call to delete
far off daughter's line,
No credit for unused lines,
No, we can't refund,

She says watch your breath, relax your jaw,
The yoga teacher, beautiful, flawless,
Perfect young woman.
Exhale, slowly, curl in like a retreating puppy,
Now inhale and arch your back like an angry cat,
Drop to sleeping child, watch your breath, don't hold
(not the customer service representative),
Namaste, Namaste, ohm,

a 25- dollar refund, (not the yoga teacher)
Says the agent in Missouri she

Used to live near you.
Laughing baby.

Namaste. Thank you
For your help. Both of you.

Thinking about Impeachment, Turning Base*

Turning base over u-pick tomato fields,
Flashback Watergate hearings, growing
My own tomatoes after grad school:
Did we get the right villains then?
Before CNN began covering stories
With a pillow until
They stopped moving,
Someone said. Or made up, shouting
New ones.
Oh, I've marched against a lot of wrongs.

Begin descent past the water tower now,
Reduce speed, flaps, runway looks lush

"*Impeachment*" studied in some fourth- grade civics text,
No Common Core indoctrinations yet, (no civics now)
the word's center, smell Georgia's
luscious evocation of southern juicy fruit, or re-configured, little elves
singly striving to signify, come on, play! Look at the word!
But yesterday the word
Boomeranged me back to Nixon,
not impeached, but resigned before it;
One article of impeachment against him, use of IRS to harass political
Enemies, sounds Stalinesque, scary.
A long time ago.
Right now it's tax time. I won't think
About peaches or "each imp meant."
Lois Lerner & Co with her successors spied.
Did they hear what I thought?

---

*   *turning base is the third leg of the aircraft landing pattern, descending before final approach and landing.*

Best keep these
opinions to myself, look over
my shoulder, turn base, descend,
the last leg before
Final approach.

Call for Peace after Election Day

Let us honor the space
Between our clenching
And our surrender,
Between our fears
And our faith
Between our obsessions
And our disciplines
Between our beliefs
And our acceptance
Whether the money,
Power is generated
Or shared,
Whether the weak
Must sink or swim
Or receive rescue rings,
Whether the just shall reign
Or wait in line,
Whether we follow left media
Or right cyberspace,
Whether evil shall rise
Or be crushed, or mollified;
We are the products of
Such different life lessons;
May we listen better,
cherish differences of perception
our tenderness for
space between us open
honorable
free.

Blood red moon: Lunar Eclipse Early Morning

On a wide clean bed, naked at moonset,
Mist hovering over the sunrise,
The shadow crept across
A perfect full moon, first caressing away
Its sharp edges, then gently nudging whiteness
Until blood flowed to nourish
Tantalized light, its partially draped
Skin flushed, and
Gradually, almost imperceptibly, the
Drape over bright senses fell
Almost completely, a rush of joy,
That curved sliver of pink, then down;
Soon, the sun's warmth
evaporated fog, her yellow
spirit flooded the sleepy room
and the wide clean bed.

Fireflies and Farewells: The Scotsman's Camp

Decades, generations at this cliff-side
family camp,
fortress command of Lake Champlain,
bagpipes after the funerals
(not all of them, actually,
suicide was quiet)
canon fire, unseen disasters, victories
defeat despair,
friends whose lives,
hurled flat-smooth stones
skipping over waves,
climbed
or descended
mad spirals, leapt,
bounced, plummeted
wind driven or
black water swallowed.

Ghosts linger to coax
redemption,
lend credence to
laughter's gifts:
Mimi's garden,
sedum and day lilies,
horses in the pasture,
sailboats anchored
parties in the barn.
Where are
all those babies?
Waves lick slippery
slate shore.
Framed by cedar,
fireflies flicker
farewell.

Saturn's Sea Water Inferred: We Are Moving Inland to Inferred Water

My sea rolls and roils today, southwest humid flow
sprays surf,
coaxes spring blooms from sand, beach daisies smile
in sea oats dunes;
the New York Times reports
a newly discovered sea on a "cue ball shiny moon" of
Saturn, where "ice crystals geyser up" from its south pole.
I contemplate my impending move inland, forever,
becoming waterless, rudderless, a dustball
dancing the wind like the ping of a disappeared jetliner,
distress in a slapping halyard from the old sailboat.

I read my grandfather's NYT obit, yellowed dusty clipping from that
same paper, nearly 70 years ago, on
the same day intrepid Lindbergh resigned from
the air corps in protest of FDR

Another crumbly headline shows a cartoon of Hitler's advance
across Eastern Europe with FDR smiling:
"Germans March on Ukraine, Nazis encircle Kiev, Russians flee"

Today the Russians are back, taking Crimea's people and seas,
some smiling president sees allies, appease please
My friend frantically arranges return airfare
for her Jewish son, but not for his new Ukrainian wife.
Today, Iraq and Iran aim missiles at one tiny democracy nearby defending
its nuclear facilities alone.
Here at home,
Thousands rush to our borderless hope. Profit-seekers avert their eyes,
Invent moral rationales.

Space travel dreams a childhood idea for Americans now.

Elon Musk and Jeff Bezos perhaps someday, unless floating Pacific
island feeds;
Still, I love the launches, sending Teslas to space, indeed.

Saturn's seas are "Inferred", the Times says, NASA's craft cannot "exactly
discern water",
but it's mapping, seeking "building blocks for life."
What if there's no water? We are moving inland. My seas will now be
inferred, too.
We've become flood insurance refugees, but we also seek water,
our "building blocks for life."

Relocation is so intense, air-conditioned,

adrift in these airless, waterless waves.

Never enough cartons. What to save,
what to cast overboard?

I mean, bury.

Sparks (Inspired by Leonard Shlain's physics and art)

If they give you an either/or choice,
Consider something new entirely,
A spark in the dark
Dichotomies are not
Opposites are not
Space/time, left/right
Art/physics, mind/universe
Red/blue
Do not imagine your own truth precludes its opposites
Do not force either/or on another
With me/against me is an illusion
Embrace the humility and Einstein awe,
The paradoxes of Bohr.
Music has been converted
into pure light, you see,
and the opposite too.
Light is not just a metaphor.
Newton proclaimed, "the largest
and strongest light corpuscles carry red,
the least bent by the prism."
Red/brown
the predominant color of art
Pre -1860,
(fire/earth, warmth/safety, light/darkness
Birth blood/heart red)

Blue comes later
(Used blood is blue veins, racial memory,
imprints, resist the cold, ice-blue,
Water/glacier/flood/sky/lightning strike blue)
Bunsen, blue flames hottest

All power to the spectrum.
Hail the invisible, enjoy don't obey
the prism. Embrace
the holy,
the transubstantiate of
light into
music.

Road Not Taken: Skyward

Rarely has anything pulled her away
from the open road's lure
the windshield's streaks
between endless crucifix
country road warnings,
bloody swales along the side,
a place every soul
has passed, storm clouds
boiling ahead;
oh, the sea's lure,
sure, its many moods,
its timelessness,
varied rhythms,
but the sky is outer
space and God, its
preciousness and variety,
untethered lift from
from digging
weeds that always
return stronger,
from others' needs she
cannot satisfy,
not freedom exactly,
as in Joplin's
*nothing left to lo*se,
rather meditation
weightless
on wind
something like
going home
wherever that is

TURNING BASE TO FINAL

"Alas It Was To None But Me"?*

Dad was miserable when I put him in the assisted living facility; he took no interest when I tried to hang his Navy memorabilia, his awards, his family photos. He couldn't get the catheter hooked up, and the nurse said he'd have to learn to do it himself, otherwise he'd have to go to a nursing home. I tried, but I couldn't do it either. A former school principal, now 89, he continually gazed across the pond at the elementary school, wondering if they needed him. Then he'd ask for the car keys I'd hidden. I went into the bathroom and vomited. My alcoholic brother skulked around the parking lot, refusing to help or speak or enter the facility. I drove back home sobbing. The next day's visit, Dad was calm at our lunch, flirting with ladies. He checked his watch the way he always had when he wanted me to go. The next day's visit, he was in the hospital dying; my brother was once again (still?) in the parking lot. We hugged, our goodbyes done. I went back into the hospital with Dad; it was a long couple of weeks. A memorial. A phone call, a road trip, and a single hospital visit to my brother, now anesthetized in a different way. The nurse opened the window, she said, for his soul to escape. One month later, I spread two bags of ashes over Tampa Bay, father and son. We sang THE PARTING GLASS, and the Navy Hymn; I danced an Irish jig on the boat deck; my brother's 3 sons and my children drank, sang and played music all night.

---

*   *The form is an attempt to emulate Jennifer Knox, Poem a Day, February 11, 2014, and the title is lyrics from "The Parting Glass", famous Irish tune. ("Of all the harm that ere I did, alas it was to none but me.")*

Pantomime on the Doomed Mango Tree

Holding my breath, I peek through aged windows:
the contractor, man in the wheelchair, waving wildly about
task's enormity, of removing the lovely tree
under which he enjoys shade relief in 98 degrees,
pantomimes root structure, canal seawall threat,
cost of project, and how soon it must be done.
One crippled arm wiggles, an atrophied root, the other
reaches as though grabbing from beneath.
A young man stands on the seawall, shoulders
drooping, silent, grudging.
He does the work.

For years, I have watched and waited each summer
for these mangos, unspeakably delicious, rare
fruit, like nothing in any store, neighbors
begging for a few, eyeing the grapefruit-sized
rosy warm messages from heaven's market. I creep into
the cluttered garage, eavesdrop as they move along,
hear the audio, finally, and the sentence
pronounced upon another old man, a world traveler,
a hopeful diplomat, who planted this tree seventy years ago:
It's gotta go.

Make way for the millionaire tourists with
McMansions to rent weekly. "Get a second opinion,"
I whisper to the universe. Maybe the
man's handicap taints his view. Pain
changes perception.
Maybe he's a mango hater.

Loss and grief are easier in pantomime,
from distance; one year later,

a neighbor Facebooked a picture
of the empty lot,
"to be built" sign, now 2.2 million
where once the taproot
anchored summer.

Sea Turtle Prescience

Waves, sea foam dreams
dressed in seaweed
And shells' sharp edges
Roll me out of bed, daybreak, onto
The beach, massive flippers tracked
laboriously, sea turtle nest,
my fingers reaching
Elbow-deep into thrown sand, seeking
Prehistoric rebirth, that
Ancient symbol of beginnings,
rubbery sea turtle egg cache,
Stored deep with hope by
Aching 300- pound mothers
Whose memories of their own
Nests rest deep in primeval centers,
Imprinted, and perhaps the egg I
Touched, wakeful sleeping, is one
Of a thousand to return
Here, to this Gulf stillness, for our children
Decades ahead
And their children
from waves, sea foam dreams
Dressed in seaweed
as memories hover
when visiting fancy hotel
aquariums, captive sea turtles
circling synthetic sand
seeking seafoam dreams
a place to nest

COLLAGE ON MY BIRTHDAY: 3 FEET BY 6 FEET, MIXED MEDIA, MULTI-DIMENSIONAL

A special glue and
finishing lacquer, perhaps, one
barrier to my finished *me* collage
its "thingness", its "ness"; my ness:
Sea oats form a large circle, superimposed triangle
pine twigs, and cedar firms the base. Layer
scores of *Sonata Pathetique*, or Bach, Joel or Joplin, scattered news headlines;
spray misty, as over the island early morning glow; brass medallions
'to thine own self', and others, center, then drawings all childlike:
upper right, a trowel, flowerpot,
handprints of three small children on a heart,
sketch mother/daughter photo swinging on a chair, ("ness" of nostalgia)
representation of son with kite, guitar, speedboat ("ness of laughter?")
stick figure family dancing at outdoor music, an Apple on desk (product placement?)
upwind sailboats, midway, waves drawn like a child, I repeat;
a scuba mask beneath, bottom corner, angel fish,
photo, white beach, full moonlight across, baby loggerheads
inching toward
Indistinct horizon; watercolor skyscape top, like The Simpsons:
airplane wings above wispy clouds,
my propeller tip touches *purpleblue* periwinkle sky, lots of it, turning base,
photo: a silver flute diagonally perched on a piano, left center
photo: books on a kayak paddle, right center
a few bullet casings, a 38 say, not a 9mm, beside a tiny bullseye target, bottom right.;

finally, bottom left,

rusty beach bicycle wheel,
with little poems in between spokes,

those spaces that vanish with
Too rapid motion.

Choose Velcro

Believing the hype of adult reassurance - you
can do any any any thing you set your mind to -
your small hands eagerly imitate tying
your new black with white logo Nikes, yes
child labor produced, but your thumbs
betray you, refuse the brain's instructions,
the result a limp black spaghetti piled atop
your small foot: instant despair. The clock
says time for school, hurry.
You, small human, must learn the tragic tricks of time,
the intense capture, recapture, of moments wasted in haste,
the painful repeat, practice, halting, revising.
You've begun. A lesson learned yesterday, a treasure
to witness, a discovery of white key between black,
specifically, finger two of the right hand, repeatedly straying to E flat,
or D flat, finally found its D, to finish *Ode to Joy*.

You will learn the knots with time, practice, the tying, looping, rabbit
through the hole, round the tree, back through the hole, or the tree
first, twice.
Perhaps to tie, then untie a small sailboat someday.
Adults aren't lying, exactly, about setting your mind to achieve
Any- any - anything. Priorities. Choose. Choose?

Perhaps choose *Ode to Joy* first. And Velcro instead of laces for just
this moment. Yes, yes, I know. Why not both?

AND SO, SOMETIMES JUST SIX WORDS:

1. A late-night host just proclaimed all late- night hosts intelligent, boosting a political project called, "Pod Save America." God is unfashionable now. We are much too intelligent for that. We prefer our own existential angst until it is unbearable, and then we write it down. I have friends who swear by red wine, and Hemingway hangovers. Blog it. Drunk blog it. Facebooktwitterinstagram it, or secret notebook in the cloud. Roseanne ambien-tweeted. Angst feels too frightening in our heads, zinging around intricate neural networks, bouncing off other universes, tumbling through black vacuums, freefall from cold suns, but look, there's no choice. It must out, onto the page. See, here on the page, it is nothing. A moonbeam.
2. I read about a young woman's rejection of childbirth's path, running marathons, an admitted addiction; it spurred my piano reflection. It's ok if I never play in public; if I stumble in six flats. It is my marathon, my method for straight-jacketing the flying monkeys with red capes catapulting between my ears. "Take Five" was impossible just a month ago for me. I discovered it is the bridge building, between one measure and the next, training left fingers to remember how far to reach, how hard to push, when the right ring finger hits G flat, skidding up to A flat, and then, surprise A natural, and C flat. Who writes a C flat? Why not just write the damn B? Acceptance, you see. Probably it was written *after* first performance, not before. Resist Googling to find out. Write now. Perhaps it keeps me from meddling in my children's lives. Co-dependency kills. It is perhaps God.
3. The child lured from his mother recognizes evil, but has no language to explain. From the corner, he watches a clenched fist fly near his mother's jaw, knows rage. When he is asked to explain, no words. Decades pass. I am helpless to repair another's life. Universal fear. Powerlessness. It is why God.
4. In the email, a sales pitch about mind/body links. Seriously? My earliest memory of powerless illness: a fever, a sore throat, swollen glands, black bean soup with lemon smile, heated by myself on a stove at 7, ginger ale, a small child's record player with yellow "vinyl" (they call it now) 45 records, the Pied Piper story, a lame

child left behind as the wondrous portals opened wide, and all the children went inside, except one, limping and sick like me, left alone. In my solitary pink frilly room on the 3rd floor, I sobbed. We didn't have cell phones, nor phones in a child's room, nor Skype, text, or Facetime, then. "She shall be as sick as she chooses," I heard my mother tell my father at day's end. I sat on the piano bench, shoulders back, chest out, and practiced Fur Elise again. Again. Again. School tomorrow, I hoped, where I'd pretend to learn for others' approval. Marathon. Suit up. I grew that day. It is *how* God.

5. Song to a sick daughter: Too fragile now to do what I could before, it is now your turn, my love, to meditate. That point in the farthest distance, a solitary dot that God will arrange, together with other dots, to create, re-arrange as art, all those neurons, electrons synesthesia somehow into color, shape, light, music. I am the dot, you are the other dot as far away as one can see. I text: Chicken soup, or black bean with lemon, honey tea, pray we meet again. Amazon pantry instead of flowers. I dare not get close to this flu. Particle theory, dot pointillism, such shabby explications for love and powerlessness, longing. I wish I could sit on the piano bench with you and our boy. Seek your own God soon.

6. Before a feast with my son and daughter-in-law, I require myself to bounce on a trampoline in a room full of trampolines in a place called "Altitudes", though I'd misread it as Attitudes. I have signed away electronically all claims illegally, since I am not my granddaughter's legal guardian. The pretty teen Cuban clerk first sells only one ticket, is embarrassed that I meant to bounce myself, fears offense taken. I laugh, intimations of mortality notwithstanding and try to imagine what she sees. I tell her I pilot airplanes, which is true. I have my pride. I pretend to myself that my sprained ankle is better now. But the bouncing whisks my breath away, like a runaway balloon, requires far more strength than I planned, is exhilarating like dance, exhausting like Zumba, mind clearing like marathon running or piano or sailing or flying or helmetless biking, terrifying like watching your child inch toward a mountain cliff edge, roughhouse near a woodstove, leave town, lose a beloved partner, drink too much, or face the courts.

7. Before dinner, we play Tom Petty songs together, matching piano, guitar, sound track. Salvation is always music. Dinner, perfectly tender chicken breasts topped with Buffalo mozzarella, sautéed garlic, halved plum tomatoes and Kalamata olive balsamic reduction, pasta and salad. The red wine bottle reads, "Hope's End: Run Away to the Dark Side to a place called Port Misery, South Australia." She is a teacher, too, like my daughter, like me, and this is a school night. I am no longer free to indulge in the remedy, but I am glad the solace works for her. As the evening progresses, we sink into (argued) politics and religion in front of a nine -year- old, who disappears to her room. We laugh at the end, agree to disagree. God, I think. I need not win. On the interstate ride home, I listen to a novel about child stealing.

8. Tiptoeing into the bedroom, still midnight rolling, I pull my feet out of tall suede boots, massage the sharp ankle pain. My ticket out of the early morning exercise class, I think. I crawl in quietly, cherish mumbled *gladyurbac*k and fall asleep. Awake, not much later, to pre-superbloodmoonlight, I move on stage, (headphones the gift) playing F, G, D minor, B flat, the rhythm just right, matching gentle snores in the next room. Then write. How poets pray when they're full. Sacred exhalations. Rotate that ankle. Flex, stretch. Not bad. Await the dawn.

9. Huge red sci-fi planet, rising from the trees, clouds parting just in time, shift the 2001 Space Odyssey Soundtrack to a bluegrass "I Draw Slow" number from the spring festival in North Carolina. Heartrate fills in gratitude. Resist sharing texts, groupthink emoticons, the twittergooglefacebookgram. Be still. This must suffice for the next superbloodmoon, the appearance of which will preside over a world without me. *Please help me. Thank you. Amen.*

Dust in the Wind, Silver Alert

Not because I want to. It is the desperate necessary game
I play to ward off the ultimate loneliness
aging human woman (how dare you select so simple
a gender in these times?)
my offspring already
assume my madness, whose political
diaspora spans three quarters century
(hey, even Brennan, former CIA Director was once
a member of the Communist Party)

this madwoman knows the totalitarian bullying of
power, left and right, sees ruin of institutions
for which she's dedicated her life
beside those she's fought to help

a silencing of speech here, a shout down there

a violent history re-write offensive, blind tongue cutting

laments the continual war against anything Judeo-Christian,
the support of anything else, victimhood delineations
that drumbeat social warrior manipulation
guilt by association you privileged white thing
never brown enough, but compassion point of view
now deemed appropriation.

I remember the look in my father's eyes
that last moment, mouth forming a howl
to speak, unable to utter the last word
in his hospital bed, a mathematician,
historian, writer, educator, social liberal, patriot,
war hero, what did he say?

Maybe it was: why didn't you bring
me a reuben sandwich, why didn't you
get your brother in here one last time,
where's Norma, (his third wife)?

Maybe it was: it just doesn't matter

any of it, and I'm only 90, I don't want to go

maybe it was: everything's gonna be all right

maybe it was: I feel as I did when my ship went
down in the Alleutians, winter 1943, bone cold weary

maybe it was: does anybody need an experienced school principal?

maybe it was: don't worry your brother is executor

(because he didn't know his son was to follow him

in a month's time, the DUI lawyers lapping up executor's money)

maybe it was: you all said there'd be this great light

maybe it was: you understand without the atomic bomb drops in
Hiroshima, Nagasaki

you probably wouldn't be

alive?

maybe it was: I'm proud to be an American where at least I know I'm free

maybe it was: I'm sorry about that Gentlemen's Agreement thing in
real estate

maybe it was: did Google really put Nazi algorithm link in "search" to Republican Party in California?
(no, that's impossible- there was no Google algorithm then)

maybe it was: life has been long and good; is there a god?

maybe it was: *Remember When* I was a full professor? Did you save my columns?

maybe it was: I'm sorry I drank so much, so late to sobriety

maybe it was: you look just like your mother

maybe it was: at least I shot my age in golf

more likely it was:

where

did you hide

my car keys?

Diode: Family Communication

Perhaps the conduit,

the converter, ac to dc,

the one-way sort of translation,

current guided

and directed, controlled

appeals like, say, arranged marriage

or purchased family compounds

representing hopeless channels

of repetition, mistakes,

current, just a mass

of rushing electrons

forced to change,

instead

of the reasoned natural miracle

power

it was intended to be.

Acknowledgements

I do not believe I have an original thought in my brain. Everything I write is a response to stimuli from all senses, generations of writers and storytellers before whom I kneel. I write from the nurture and challenge of students and teachers with whom I've shared my journey thus far, from family, group and community members who suffered my membership, from all my mothers and sisters. I devour work of many famous poets, writers, and artists whose encouraging, inspiring rudders guide in recovery from an often dizzying, existential, freefall spin. My best friend's little airplane that I fly, an old Piper Tomahawk called "Shadowfax", (after Gandolf's horse in Tolkien's Lord of the Rings), is often referred to as a "Trauma-hawk," because of its "spinning" capability. It was designed to teach pilots how to get out of a downward spiral, or spin. Perhaps writing is the same thing for me. Survival. My deepest gratitude to all who encourage poetry. I'm turning base, after all.

Even fully aware of my offspring's comment, "Mom, why do you write all that crap?", the vague answer has something to do with wind, and breath.

Paraphrases and references in letter poem, "Dear Nikky Finney" from Head Off & Split,
Northwestern University Press, 2011, p. 3, and p. 72.

Quotes and paraphrase in poem of address, "Avocation 3: Billy Collins"
Horoscopes for the Dead
Random House, 2012, from "Vocation", p. 55
and
Hislop, Susanna

p. 104 "A True Story About an Insignificant Northern Constellation"
Stories in the Stars,
Penguin Books, 2015

Discussion in "Saturn Water Inferred", from The New York Times, April 3, 2014, Science section

Discussions in several poems on quantum physics, time and light, refer to
Shlain, Leonard
Art and Physics: Parallel Visions in Space, Time and Light
Harper Collins, 2001

Disney and Dali Exhibit
Dali Museum
St. Petersburg, FL
Spring, 2015
"Viola Organista" is a response to an online concert viewed here:
http://www.violaorganista.com See also: https://www.facebook.com/ViolaOrganista First performance of the viola organista made by Sławomir Zubrzycki. INTERNATIONAL ROYAL CRACOW PIANO FESTIVAL 18TH OCTOBER 2013, Aula Florianka.

Reference to Wallace Stevens' poem, "Sunday Morning", PoetryFoundation.Org, accessed Feb. 24, 2018

References to Nicole Calahan and Jennifer Knox from "Poem-a-day.org", April 11, 2014.

References to *Narrative* Magazine, January 2017.

References to "God Bless the USA," song by Lee Greenwood, 1984, from album "You've Got a Good Love Comin'", accessed Wikipedia, June 1, 2018

References to "Dust in the Wind", song by Kansas, 1977, "Point of Know Return" album written by Kerry Livgren, Voice Steve Walsh, Violin and Viola Robby Steinhardt, information accessed Wikipedia, June 1, 2018

Poem, "Humanitarian", first published NCTE April, 1995

References to *I Remember When* column
in Englewood Sun newspaper, William Mullen, 1980s -1990s

Epilogue about Billy Graham

- see, perhaps, the article by a South Bronx native Jewish writer, Steve Posner, *Billy Graham and Me editor,* suggesting how Billy Graham wanted us to be purple, not red and blue, highlighting his insistence on integrated crusades and revivals.
- https://www.google.com/url?sa=t&rct=j&q=&esrc=s&source=web&cd=3&cad=rja&uact=8&ved=0ahUKEwjIjM79gbrbAhXM6J8KHd9lCvoQFgg-2MAI&url=https%3A%2F%2Fwww.nationalreview.com%2F2018%2F03%2Fbilly-graham-evangelical-leader%2F&usg=AOvVaw2XkaKRtpbmBgMfqgpDbUZj accessed March 1, 2018

Further preparation:

About the author, *in her own words*:

Writing has always been my needful obsession, both cathartic and joyful.

I read, teach, play piano, fly airplanes, sail some, garden, kayak, travel, love a few very deeply, but writing is my center. I've lived in many places, though most of my work is rooted in the Northeast and Florida. Overseas teaching (China, three summers, and Guatemala, one, Chile one) strengthened my spiritual center. I've also been active in a recovery program for decades.

My first literary love is poetry, and I've devoted most of my life to studying it, enjoying it, and making it accessible to others in one way or another. I participated in Bread Loaf Writers' Conference in '94, the Geraldine R Dodge Poetry Festival, the Peoples' Poetry Gathering in NYC, Poetry Out Loud, and Eckerd College Writers in Paradise, and "Poetry Alive" as a teacher/coach. I've given several poetry readings and published a few poems (one in the NCTE Journal -) in small journals over the years. Most recently, I attended the San Miguel de Allende Writers Conference and Literary Festival, a delightful inspiration, and usually attend the Florida Writers Association, and the Association of Writers and Poets conferences.

With a BA in English from Binghamton University, a MS from University at Albany, additional graduate work at McGill, SUNY Plattsburgh, (former) St. Michael's College in Burlington, Vt., and Indiana University, I've taught English and ESL at public middle schools, high schools, prisons, and colleges for over 40 years.

Six years ago, I got my private pilot's license in Sarasota, and discovered a phenomenal world of imaginative layers, possibilities and existence. My beloved partner Ed, a pilot, teacher, Master Craftsman, is the best human being on the planet. My beautiful adult children and grandchildren, just an hour away from our airplane community in Florida, write new stories of innovation and achievement daily. A full life of children, step-children, dear friends, in-laws, outlaws, students, writing souls, neighbors, enthusiasts, flyers, divers, and givers creates in me a gratitude well beyond words.

EPILOGUE

THE REVEREND BILLY GRAHAM IS DEAD

"Just As I Am", the soothing choir sang softly, four part harmony for Dr. Graham's call, "Come forward, offer your heart to Jesus." A child, I was not so much moved as wanting to move, to follow the smiling people, some weeping, toward waiting helpers, and to glimpse closer those angels, down the aisle, down, closer to center. My mother, so beautiful, smiled at me, tears in her eyes, and suddenly my father was not so angry. Both took me by the hand to go forward at Madison Square Garden. It was magic. I was so filled with love and security and protection and hope.

(My older brother had ducked the trip, and he would always later say that Dad only went because he was hoping to get laid. A cynical sort, my brother, though possibly correct.)

But they took me to a room of instruction, too many words too late at night, away from the music, the power. My father grew restless, checking his watch, and once again, my parents were unhappy. The ride home along the LI expressway was sad and tense. Considering this, and my subsequent experiences with church, adding a horror that my Jewish best friend would not be admitted to the Kingdom of Heaven, the words of instruction slipped away. But not the music, the power, the light.

People resent this man, Billy Graham, a poor white boy who became chaplain to powerful people in highly divisive times of change. I'm out of time for culture war resentments.* Sure, I have plenty. But Billy Graham urged us to open those clenched fists, palms up, to hand off those resentments to something greater, to let them go.

The simple, basic appeal of Dr. Graham's method, his message, his music, his story, lifts my spirit as the instruction room did not, does not. That moment just as I was, walking on love toward the center of Madison Square Garden, returns as resource when despair crushes, when more students and teachers are destroyed, yet another ticking time bomb we failed to defuse, another monster we failed to keep from our children. I remember powerlessness. I remember hope. I remember loving arms around my shoulders after lighting a chalice, later on. I remember playing hymns. I remember I cannot live immersed in anger. I remember long summer evenings reading verses on the Asheville, NC porch of Margaret McCune, blind social worker, a talking book miracle for mountain people. I remember nephew Andrew's 40th birthday square dance, with all my boys. I remember deep conversations with a little boy wiser than he should be, and another grown wise with pain. I remember a host of teachers who "keep on keeping on" anyway. And the gifts of despair, forgiveness. No greater joy, no greater love.

Please help us. Just as I am, oh God. Whoever or whatever or wherever you are. My friend refers to his all-knowing buddy, HUGE. Be with us. Gracias, merci, spasibo, xie xie, danka, thank you for the strength to go on, to heal, to nurture kindness. From my father's side of the family, Kyrie eleison. From my Unitarian brothers and sisters, unconditional love without divide. May it be.

www.ingramcontent.com/pod-product-compliance
Lightning Source LLC
LaVergne TN
LVHW092050060526
838201LV00047B/1318